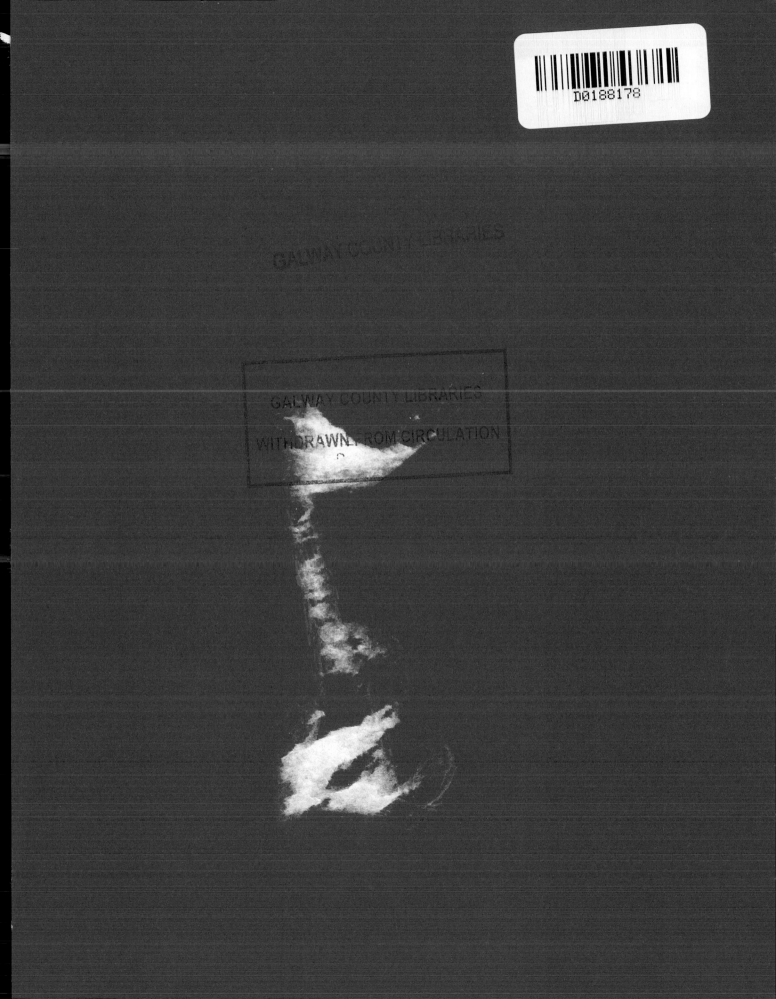

# WORLD ORGANIZATIONS

# The World Health Organization

## Jillian Powell

WORLD HEALTH ORGANIZATION

ORGANISATION MONDIALE DE LA SANTÉ

# W
## FRANKLIN WATTS
### LONDON • SYDNEY

First published in 2000
by Franklin Watts
96 Leonard Street
London EC2A 4XD

Franklin Watts Australia
56 O'Riordan Street, Alexandria
NSW 2015

Editors: Sarah Snashall, Anderley Moore
Designer: Simon Borrough
Picture research: Sue Mennell
Consultant: Gregory Hartl, WHO
Spokesperson

A CIP catalogue record for this book is
available from the British Library.

ISBN    0 7496 3691 2

Dewey classification 610.6

Printed in Malaysia

Picture credits:
Cover: WHO (copyright H. Anenden).
Inside: AKG: 7 (bottom);
Panos Pictures: 4 (bottom) 6, 13
(top), 16 (top and bottom), 17
(bottom), 18; 19 (bottom), 20
(bottom), 21, 22 (top and bottom),
23 (bottom), 24, 27 (top), 28;
Rex Pictures: 27 (bottom), 29;
Science Photo Library: 7 (top), 15,
19 (top); Still: 5, 14 (top and bottom) 23
(top); WHO (copyright H. Anenden): 4
(top), 8; 9, 11 (top and bottom), 12, 13
(bottom), 17 (top), 25.

J115, 162
£12.99

# Contents

# 1. What is WHO?

The World Health Organization (WHO) is a worldwide organization which aims to bring good health to everyone in the world. It tackles global health problems such as the lack of health education and health services and the spread of infectious and non-infectious diseases.

## Creating world health

WHO helps to improve health for people worldwide in a number of ways. It sends health experts around the world to train and support local health workers. It funds research into disease. It provides information and medical supplies to countries who are trying to create better health care systems. It gathers information about disease which can be used by people who are making decisions about health programmes. It organizes immunization programmes.

## Spotlight

'Health is a state of complete physical, mental and social well-being and not merely the absence of disease or infirmity.'
The World Health Organization

◀ Malnutrition in developing countries is a growing problem as the world population increases.

## WHO and the UN

The World Health Organization is part of the United Nations (UN) – an organization, made up of countries from around the world, which aims to bring about world peace. WHO is a specialized agency within the UN which means it is a separate organization which looks after a particular part of the aims of the UN.

▼ *A scientist, funded by WHO, carries out research on river blindness, a disease transmitted by bad water..*

### ✔ Checklist

The main aims of the World Health Organization are set out in its Constitution. WHO aims:

- To fight diseases
- To help governments improve their health services
- To improve people's nutrition, housing, sanitation, and working conditions
- To encourage scientific groups who work for health to work together
- To encourage people worldwide to meet and agree on health matters
- To encourage and carry out research on health matters
- To set international standards for foods and medicines
- To improve health education
- To collect and store data on health matters

## Setting standards

One of WHO's most important functions is publishing information about disease and setting standards for health care. This information is used by people who make decisions about health. For example, in its 'World Health Report 2000', WHO published a list of 191 countries' health systems in order of performance. Countries whose health systems come low in the list may use the information in the report to improve their system.

▶ *A child is vaccinated against polio in Senegal. As a result of WHO's immunization programmes, nearly 80 per cent of the world's children are now vaccinated against such major diseases.*

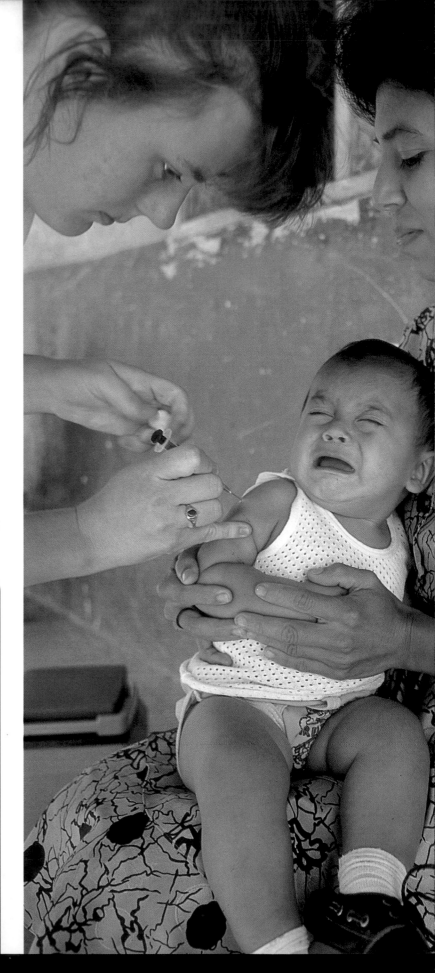

## ✓ Checklist

WHO judges a country's health system by:

- How healthy the population is
- The differences in health between rich and poor
- How well the health system treats ill people
- Whether rich and poor people receive the same standard of health care
- Whether poor people have to pay more than they can afford for health care

WHO was set up in 1948 after the Second World War. The countries which grouped together to form the United Nations after the war believed that the health of all peoples would be very important in maintaining peace and security in the future. They set up The World Health Organization to work for global health.

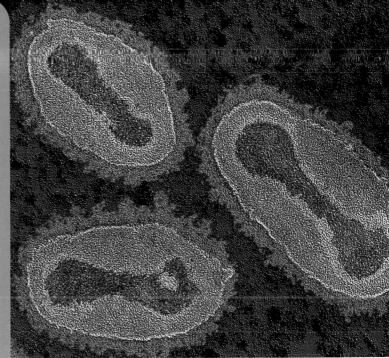

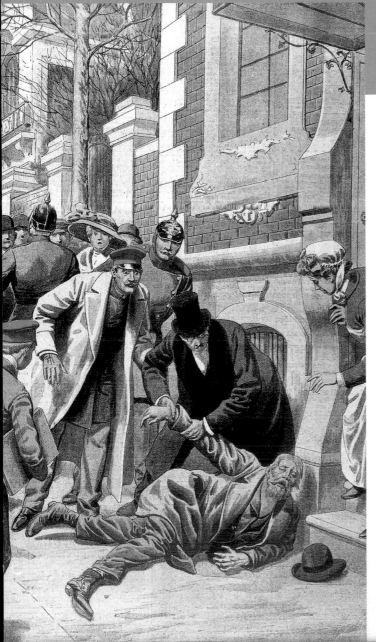

◀ A man collapses from cholera. In the 19th century, thousands of people died from cholera in Europe.

▲ The smallpox virus which was wiped out in the 1970s by WHO's immunization programme.

## Beginning

People from different countries first began to discuss public health matters in the 19th century. They discussed the spread of communicable (infectious) diseases like smallpox and cholera which were widespread at the time.

In 1851, representatives from 12 countries met at the first International Conference on Public Health, in Paris. After this and other conferences, a series of different international health organizations was set up in the US and Europe.

▲ The WHO headquarters in Geneva, Switzerland, where almost one third of WHO's staff work.

## International health

After the First World War (1914–1918), world governments grouped together to form the League of Nations in Geneva to help prevent another war. The League formed an International Health Organization in 1923. After the Second World War, when the League had broken up, the members of the newly formed United Nations met in New York to discuss setting up a new international health organization. They drafted the Constitution for the World Health Organization.

The first World Health Assembly of WHO was held on 24th June 1948.

## ✓ Checklist

Important dates in the history of WHO

| | |
|---|---|
| 1830 | Cholera overruns Europe |
| 1851 | First International Conference on Public Health is held in Paris |
| 1907 | International Office of Public Health is set up in Paris |
| 1923 | The League of Nations forms an International Health Organization |
| 1948 | The Constitution of WHO is approved in New York |
| 1948 | The First World Health Assembly is held in Geneva |
| 1980 | WHO confirms that smallpox has been wiped out worldwide |
| 1981 | WHO launches its programme of 'health for all by the year 2000' |
| 1998 | WHO celebrates its 50th anniversary |

# 3. How WHO works

Any country can belong to WHO. In 1998, on WHO's 50th anniversary, 191 countries, known as member states, belonged to WHO. All member states help decide the work that WHO will do. WHO carries out its work through three groups of people: the World Health Assembly, the Executive Board and the Secretariat.

▼ *A WHO health worker in Mauritius listens to a baby's heartbeat during an antenatal check-up to make sure that it is healthy.*

## The World Health Assembly

The World Health Assembly (WHA) is the supreme decision-making body of WHO. It holds a meeting that takes place every year in May, normally in Geneva. Representatives from all member states and from other international health organizations attend the Assembly. Its main function is to approve WHO's programme of work and budget for the next two years, and to decide on WHO's policies. Each member state has one vote at the World Health Assembly.

## The Executive Board

The Executive Board meets at least twice a year. Its work is to put into action the decisions and policies of the World Health Assembly, and to advise and support the Assembly. It prepares the agenda and programme of work for the next meeting of the Assembly. The Executive Board also decides on emergency measures to fight outbreaks of disease or other disasters.

The Executive Board is made up of 32 health experts. The WHA elects member states that will sit on the executive board. These member states then choose a health expert to sit on the board as their representative. The members of the Executive Board hold office for three years. The Board acts for all the member states.

▼ *A meeting of the Executive Board. The Executive Board meets twice a year, usually in January and again in May.*

## The Director General

The Secretariat is headed by the Director General who is nominated by the Executive Board and appointed by the World Health Assembly. The Director General is appointed for one or two five-year terms. He or she works with the eight executive directors who are responsible for the eight sections of WHO.

◀ *Dr Gro Harlem Brundtland became Director General in July 1998. She is a medical doctor and was Norway's Prime Minister before joining WHO.*

## The Secretariat

The staff of WHO – around 5000 people worldwide – is known as the Secretariat. WHO staff include medical and public health experts, nurses, chemists, economists, translators, editors and accountants. They work at the WHO Headquarters in Geneva, in the Regional Offices and on field programmes worldwide. Some work as WHO representatives in member states where they help the member government plan and manage national health programmes. They will also keep WHO informed of any special health problems in that country.

All staff members of WHO are responsible to WHO as an international organization and not to any national government.

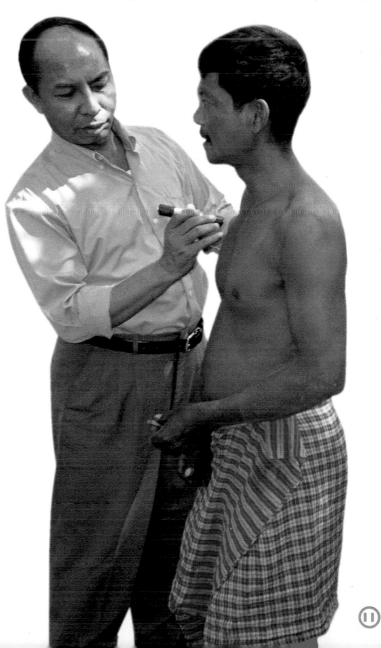

▶ *One of the doctors from WHO's Leprosy Control Programme in Cambodia examines a patient.*

## Funding

WHO is funded by fixed contributions from its members and by voluntary donations from governments. Member states contribute an amount which reflects their wealth and population. The main contributions are made by the United States, Japan, Germany, France and the United Kingdom. The United States contributes 25 per cent of WHO's budget. The poorest states contribute very small amounts.

Each year, WHO has a budget, from fixed and voluntary donations, of about $850 million (£560 million). The budget is divided between the Regional Offices and they decide how to use the funds. Over 50 per cent of WHO's budget is used in developing countries.

WHO also receives voluntary donations from governments and other United Nations agencies for specific programmes. It also receives donations of goods, such as polio vaccines, from private companies.

## Regional Offices

The member states are divided into six Regions, each of which has a Regional Office and Committee under a Regional Director. The Regional Offices are responsible for regional policies and activities. They act as a contact between WHO and the member states within each Region. Regional advisors help member governments when they request advice or support.

### Spotlight

For 15 years, the American pharmaceutical company Merck and Co. have been providing WHO with a drug to treat the disease river blindness. Since 1998, the UK company Smith Kline Beecham has been providing WHO with a drug to treat the disease elephantiasis.

### Problem

WHO must be careful when accepting donations of medicines from companies. They must be able to show that they remain in control of any programme that a private company is helping them with, and that the private company is not gaining power by helping WHO.

▼ A map showing WHO's six Regional offices and the areas they cover.

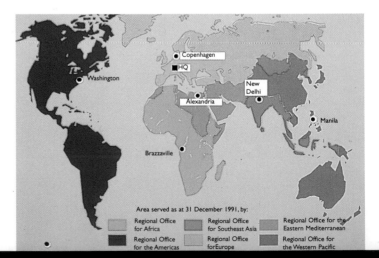

Area served as at 31 December 1991, by:

Regional Office for Africa

Regional Office for the Americas

Regional Office for Southeast Asia

Regional Office for Europe

Regional Office for the Eastern Mediterranean

Regional Office for the Western Pacific

# 4. Fighting disease

WHO works to prevent and control diseases around the world. These include communicable (infectious) diseases which can spread from person to person, like measles, polio and tuberculosis, and non-communicable diseases like cancer and heart disease.

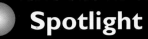
## Controlling epidemics

WHO works to prevent outbreaks of disease. It uses field technology and public health training programmes to help countries control epidemics. It is developing a network of public health centres to help countries work together to detect and control outbreaks of disease. WHO also collects and publishes information on diseases and outbreaks around the world. This information can be used to predict outbreaks or to help people who make decisions about health.

▲ A medical team takes a blood sample from a sick woman in Kenya.

When there is an outbreak of an infectious disease WHO can send field workers on site within 24 hours to put control measures in place. These health experts can help set up quarantine measures to stop the disease spreading, train local staff and investigate where and how the disease is spreading.

◀ A medical worker gives a young child a polio vaccine to protect him from the disease.

## Spotlight

Until 1967, the deadly disease smallpox killed 2 million people a year. WHO ran a ten year campaign to rid the world of smallpox, and the last known case was recorded in Somalia in 1977.

▶ A nurse bandages a leprosy patient at a clinic in Bombay, India.

## Tropical diseases

In 1999, 1.2 million people died from tropical diseases. WHO works with the United Nations Development Programme (UNDP) and the World Bank to fight major tropical diseases including malaria, leprosy and river blindness (onchocerciasis).

▲ Project workers fighting river blindness on Africa's Ivory Coast hold their monthly meeting.

WHO supports over 2,600 projects worldwide through its Programme for Research and Training in Tropical Diseases. Scientists and medical experts funded by WHO work to find better ways to diagnose and treat tropical diseases. WHO also supports local projects, such as constructing tsetse fly traps in African villages to kill the flies that carry the disease known as sleeping sickness.

## Malaria

Every year over 300 million people catch malaria – a disease carried by mosquitoes in tropical countries. WHO funds research into new drugs for malaria, into work that reduces the number of mosquitoes and into easy-to-implement measures such as bed nets soaked in insecticide to stop people being bitten by mosquitoes.

▼ *Mosquitoes pass malaria on to people by biting into the skin and feeding on blood.*

## Spotlight

In 1974, WHO worked with other United Nations agencies on a programme to control river blindness, a disease carried by flies in tropical countries, especially in Africa. The programme included spraying the river breeding grounds of the flies with insecticides. 1.5 million people have been cured of the disease by the programme and huge areas of riverside land can now be safely farmed.

## Problem

Malaria is proving difficult to wipe out because the mosquitoes that pass it to humans have become resistant to insecticides. Scientists must go on looking for new insecticides.

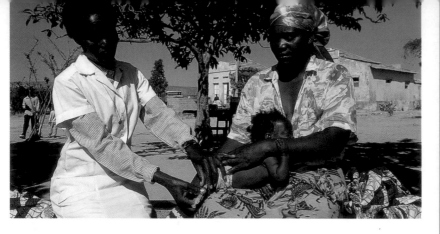

▲ *A child is immunized at a health centre in Angola.*

## Immunization

Some diseases can be prevented by immunization. These include polio (poliomyelitis), tetanus, measles, diphtheria, whooping cough and tuberculosis. Each year, 2 million children die or are disabled from these diseases because they have not been immunized. There are around 5,000 cases of polio alone every year, but this number is falling and WHO predicts that polio will be wiped out worldwide by 2005.

Since 1974, WHO has worked with the United Nations' Children's Emergency Fund, (UNICEF), to increase the number of children immunized. Nearly 80 per cent of the world's children are now immunized against common childhood diseases.

There has been a civil war in Angola for the last 20 years. In the 1990s the fighting became worse. Thousands of people were forced to become refugees in Luanda and in other cities. They settled there in makeshift shelters without clean water or sanitation. Many children had not been immunized because of the war, and this caused a major polio outbreak which paralysed 1100 children and killed 89. WHO and UNICEF organized truces in the fighting, called Days of Tranquillity, when children could be immunized.

▼ *This boy has been disabled by polio. Polio is still a common childhood disease in parts of Africa, the Eastern Mediterranean and South Asia.*

*Teenagers in a mixed high school in India are given a sex education class focusing on AIDS awareness and safe sex.*

## AIDS

AIDS is the world's biggest infectious disease killer. WHO estimates that at least 34 million people worldwide have the HIV virus that causes AIDS. WHO monitors the spread of AIDS through a network of centres worldwide.

## Drug safety

WHO sets down international standards for the quality and safety of drugs and medicines. It has produced a Model List of essential drugs and vaccines, and gives advice to member states on forming national drugs policies.

## ⬤ Spotlight

The AIDS support organization in Uganda (TASO), which is supported by WHO, provides medical care, counselling and support for patients with AIDS and their families. The organization was set up with the help of government health workers and relatives of AIDS victims. Community health workers send patients to the weekly clinics run by the organization in local hospitals.

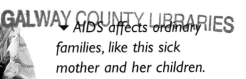

*AIDS affects ordinary families, like this sick mother and her children.*

# 5. Health education

WHO informs and educates people worldwide on health matters. Its health education programme informs people about healthy eating and lifestyle. It gives information on how some diseases can be prevented by healthy nutrition, exercise, health care and hygiene, and how to prevent accidental injuries.

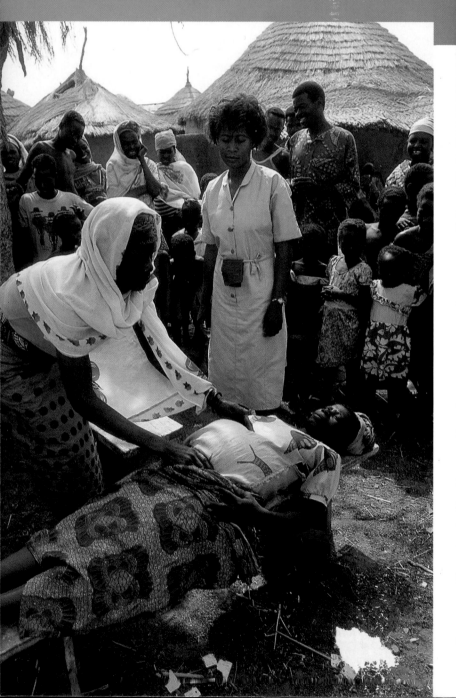

## ● Spotlight

A project in the Kheda district of Gujarat, India, trained local women to work as village family welfare workers in local communities. The project was supported by a local charity trust and by the Indian government with overseas aid and the United Nations Population Fund (UNFPA) and reached 30 villages in the district. The village family welfare workers were trained to give help and advice on topics like immunization and family planning, and to carry out home visits and prescribe basic drugs.

## Health workers

WHO staff work with community health workers, volunteers, other medical staff and local television and radio to encourage communities to work together for health. WHO spends about 10 per cent of its budget each year on training health staff. Health workers are trained in skills such as helping mothers through a healthy pregnancy and birth, and teaching good child care and nutrition.

◀ *This project in Ghana trains local women to assist in childbirth.*

## Publishing health

WHO publishes health information in books, journals and on the Internet. This includes training manuals, reports by experts, and the results of scientific studies funded by WHO. Information is published in six main languages: English, French, Spanish, Russian, Chinese and Arabic.

## Health care and diet

Many diseases, like cancer and heart disease, can be prevented by a healthy lifestyle. In developing countries, malnutrition is caused by food shortages leading to starvation or a poor diet lacking in protein, vitamins and minerals. In the industrialized world, malnutrition is usually caused by eating too many fatty and sugary foods and by over-eating. These can lead to diseases including cancer, heart disease and diabetes. WHO works to educate people to eat a healthy diet and to take regular exercise.

▲ *A health worker in Sudan informs villagers about drugs which can be used to fight river blindness*

▼ *These Bangladeshi women are learning about clean water and sanitation.*

## Spotlight

### Tobacco Free Initiative

Every year, 4 million people die from diseases caused by smoking. WHO is working on a new international convention to control tobacco production and advertising. It works to inform and educate people on the risks of tobacco smoking. It helps member states develop anti-smoking policies like banning tobacco advertising and introducing laws to ensure clean air for all.

▼ A WHO field dentist checks a boy's teeth. Dental decay and gum disease are very common diseases worldwide.

## Preventing blindness

There are about 45 million blind people in the world, and blindness is up to twenty times more common in developing countries than in the industrialized world. Two thirds of all cases of blindness could be prevented by good nutrition and eye care. WHO helps governments to set up National Blindness Prevention Programmes. These programmes teach people how blindness can be caused by a lack of vitamin A in the diet, and by eye infections which are not treated.

Some cases of blindness are caused by disease, for example the disease river blindness in Africa. WHO runs programmes to reduce the number of blackflies which cause the disease.

▶ A boy who has been blinded by river blindness.

## Mental Health Programme

In many countries, traditional ways of life are disappearing fast. Families are breaking up and people cannot rely on regular work or a happy homelife. Many people suffer mental illness as a result and some turn to alcohol or drugs which harm their health. WHO estimates that about 300 million people worldwide suffer from mental illnesses.

WHO's Mental Health Programme aims to educate people in mental health problems including alcohol and drug abuse.

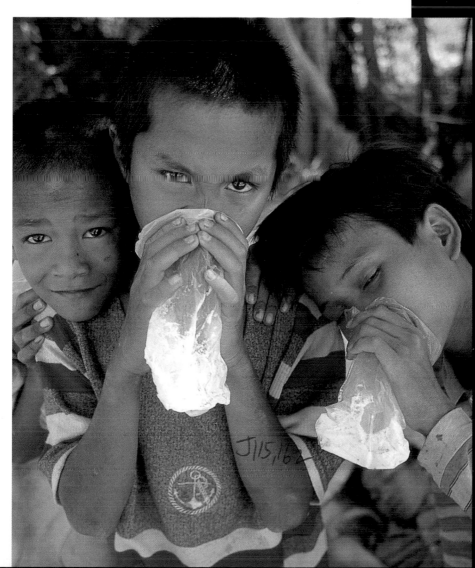

◀ *These homeless boys in Bangkok have become addicted to sniffing glue.*

# 6. Environmental health

One of the main tasks set out in WHO's Constitution is to improve environmental health. This includes the food people eat, the houses they live in, the water and sanitation facilities they use and the conditions they work in.

## Problem

WHO and FAO issue guidelines and standards for food safety. Although member states are asked to accept these standards, governments can decide whether or not to make them law.

▲ *A potato crop in Peru is sprayed with pesticides.*

## Food safety

Illness caused by eating contaminated food affects millions of people each year. WHO runs a food safety programme which helps member states improve their food safety laws and systems. It works with the Food and Agriculture Organization of the United Nations (FAO) to set safe levels for pesticides and food additives.

## Clean water

One billion people in the world do not have safe drinking water – this can lead to health problems including diarrhoea. WHO sets guidelines for safe drinking water and helps member states improve their water supplies.

## Spotlight

In 1980, only 40 per cent of people living in developing countries had access to safe drinking water, and only 20 per cent had proper toilet and washing facilities. Ten years later, WHO's Programme for Safe Water and Sanitation had doubled these figures.

▶ *Millions of people in developing countries rely on water fetched from wells.*

◀ Millions of people worldwide are homeless or live in poor shanty homes.

▼ Child labour is still used in some countries. This young boy works at a brick factory in Bangladesh.

## Decent housing

Poor housing can lead to disease and death. WHO has set up projects to study the links between health and housing and has issued guidelines to governments.

## Working conditions

Two thirds of all workers around the world work in poor conditions. Every year, there are 33 million cases of injury at work, including hearing loss, lung and skin disease and cancer. WHO has set up a Workers' Health Programme which helps member states improve conditions at work.

## Pollution

WHO monitors how air and water pollution, and chemicals and radioactivity in the environment affect world health. It also sets up expert committees to study the effects on health of climate change from global warming and damage to the ozone hole.

# 7. Working together

WHO works closely with a range of other organizations to improve health worldwide. Many of WHO's projects are run jointly with other UN bodies, with local governments and government bodies, or with non-governmental organizations (NGOs) which include charities and private companies.

## Other UN agencies

WHO works closely with other United Nations Agencies. One of its closest partners is the United Nations Children's Fund (UNICEF). WHO and UNICEF work on joint projects including immunization, mother and child health, nutrition and sanitation. WHO works with the United Nations Development Programme (UNDP), the United Nations Population Fund (UNFPA), and the World Bank on health issues such as tropical diseases and family planning.

## Spotlight

WHO has launched a programme called 'Kick Polio out of Africa'. It is working with Rotary International and other partners to hold National Immunization Days. The campaign was launched by President Nelson Mandela and supported by the WHO goodwill ambassador, Ghanaian footballer Abedi Pélé.

▼ Boxes of vaccine are delivered to a health clinic in Mali for a programme funded by WHO and UNICEF.

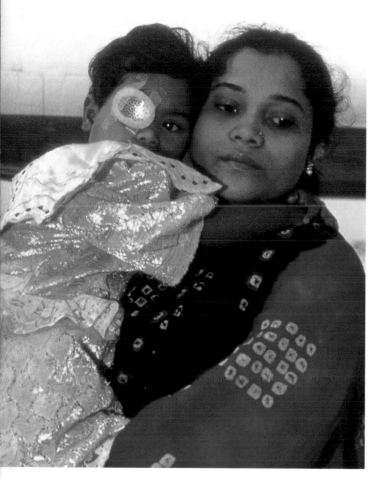

## Health institutions

Health Institutions store data and carry out scientific and technical research for WHO. WHO also works with non-governmental organizations concerned with health such as Médecins Sans Frontières (Doctors Without Borders) and ORBIS International. ORBIS works to prevent blindness and helps WHO research into numbers and causes of blindness around the world.

## Private companies

Private companies, such as makers of drugs and vaccines, also support WHO. Since 1984, WHO has worked with the International Federation of Pharmaceutical Manufacturers to fight AIDS by researching and developing new drugs and vaccines for the HIV virus.

▲ A girl leaves the ORBIS jet plane after her operation. The jet plane houses an eye hospital and teaching area. It travels around the world performing operations and training local staff.

## Problem

Some diseases like tuberculosis have become resistant to the drugs used to treat them. New drugs must be developed to prevent them from spreading again.

## Spotlight

WHO worked with the Botswana Salt Company to make sure that all salt produced in South African countries is iodized. This will help control IDDs, or iodine-deficiency disorders which can lead to disability and death in young children. The Project was supported by local governments as well as UNICEF and the International Council for the Control of IDD.

## Relief work

WHO works with other organizations and governments to help people in emergencies such as wars or natural disasters. WHO works with the United Nations High Commissioner for Refugees (UNHCR), UNICEF and other agencies to provide drugs, vaccines and other medical supplies for the refugees. WHO sends technical experts who work with the medical teams in the field to supply clean water, food and immunization against diseases such as cholera and measles. The WHO experts will also monitor the relief aid given for quality. WHO member states may be asked to send medical supplies to the area.

## ● Spotlight

Hurricane Mitch was the worst cyclonic storm ever to hit the Atlantic basin. In 1998, it devastated five Central American countries, affecting 3.3 million people. WHO's task forces were working in the area within 48 hours to assess health risks and problems. WHO called for international help to restore health services and to fight the threat of communicable diseases spreading from unsafe water and sanitation.

▼ *Relief workers come to the aid of injured people in a city that has been hit by a hurricane in Peru, South America. Special teams provide medical help and counselling.*

# 8. Future challenges

WHO and other health organizations have been successful in improving health worldwide. This has led to an increase in world population figures. There are now over 6 billion people in the world. This increase in population brings new health challenges in the 21st century.

▲ Every country must find ways of caring for an ageing population. This is an old people's home in Mozambique.

▼ Jean Marie Calmont on her 121st birthday. In the 21st century, many people are expected to live over the age of 100.

## Living longer

By 2025, most children will be fully immunized and science will have conquered more diseases. Better nutrition and health care mean that people will be living longer. Fifty years ago, the average lifespan was 48 years. By 2025 people can expect to live for an average 73 years. In richer, industrialized countries, many babies born in the year 2000 will live over 100 years.

## Ageing populations

By 2025, there may be 1.2 billion people over the age of 60. As the world's population grows older, health systems face new challenges. To raise awareness of this, WHO has launched a global movement for 'Active Ageing'.

## Future problems

WHO predicts that: non-communicable (non-infectious) diseases will become more common in the future; more people will live in unhealthy housing; an increase in pollution may lead to more deaths from heart and lung diseases; damage to the ozone layer may increase cases of skin cancer.

Many infectious diseases remain a growing threat to world health. WHO predicts that malaria will become a larger problem in the future as global warming leads to more mosquitoes and as political problems cause a breakdown in health systems.

Mental health problems will also increase in the future. WHO predicts that in the year 2050 the stress-related mental health condition, depression will become the world's second largest form of disability.

*Traffic congestion and pollution cause major health problems in central Taipei, Taiwan.*

## Problem

Developing countries carry 90 per cent of the world's diseases but have only 10 per cent of its health care resources.

## Technology and health

Advances in technology are also raising new health issues. It is now possible for women in their 50s and 60s to give birth to a child, but many people believe it is not fair for children to be born to much older mothers.

Scientists have also found out how to clone, or copy, living material from plants and animals. Cloning living material could help cure people of diseases but many people are opposed to the idea of cloning humans. They are worried that we will lose the idea of people as individuals and that clones may just be used for medical purposes or spare parts for surgery.

### Checklist

Major Health issues for the 21st century

- The impact of new technology
- Environmental pollution
- Poor nutrition and tobacco smoking
- Ageing and increased populations
- Non-communicable diseases
- Stress-related mental health problems

WHO has formed expert committees to discuss the issues that are being raised by the new technology.

## Health and the Internet

It is now possible for medical ideas and products to be traded all over the world on the Internet. WHO has formed working groups with the European Union to set out new rules and regulations for the sale of medical products and services on the Internet.

### Problem

The Internet gives millions of people access to medical products and services but there is a danger that unsafe products or ideas could come onto the market.

◀ *Having given birth aged 63, this woman is the world's oldest new mother.*

# Glossary

**Antibiotics**    drugs used to fight infections caused by germs

**Collaborating health centres**    health centres that work with WHO

**Communicable**    the word used for a disease which can be passed from one person to another

**Constitution**    a formal document setting up a new organization which outlines its structure and activities

**Contaminated**    when something is dirty or unsafe

**Developing countries**    countries that are still becoming industrialized

**Epidemics**    a widespread outbreak of disease

**Food additives**    chemicals that are added in food production

**Governing body**    a group or organization of people that takes decisions on major issues

**Malnutrition**    a diet which is poor or inadequate

**Non-communicable**    the word used for diseases which cannot be caught

**Nutrition**    everything that makes up a diet

**Pandemics**    outbreaks of disease affecting entire regions or even the whole world

**Primary health care**    providing essential health services and helping individuals and communities work for health

**Quarantine**    a period of time in which people or animals who might spread disease are kept away from others.

**Tropical**    belonging to the area of the Tropics, near the Earth's Equator

**Ultrasound**    Technology that uses sound waves to see inside things for example, to see a baby inside its mother's womb.

# Useful addresses

**Offices of the World Health Organization:**
**WHO Headquarters:**
World Health Organization
20 Avenue Appia
CH-1211 Geneva 27, Switzerland

**WHO Regional Offices:**
WHO Regional Office for Africa
(Temporary address)
Medical School, C Ward
Parirenyatwa Hospital, Mazoe Street
PO Box BE 773, Belvedere
Harare, Zimbabwe
www.whoafr.org

WHO Regional Office for the Americas/Pan
   American Sanitary Bureau
525 23rd Street N.W.
Washington, D.C. 20037, USA
www.paho.org

WHO Regional Office for the Eastern
Mediterranean
PO Box 1517, Alexandria 21511, Egypt
www.who.sci.eg

WHO Regional Office for Europe
8, Scherfigsvej
DK-2100 Copenhagen O, Denmark
www.who.dk

WHO Regional Office for South-East Asia
World Health House
Indraprastha Estate, Mahatma Gandhi Road
New Delhi 110002, India
www.whosea.org

WHO Regional Office for the Western Pacific
PO Box 2932
Manila, 1000 Philippines
www.wpro.who.int

**Other WHO Web Sites:**
• **www.who.int**
Home page for WHO(OMS)

• **www.unsystem.org**
Directory of United Nations web sites

• **www.unaids.org**
Web site for the UN campaign against AIDS

• **www.who.int/ina-ngo**
Directory of non-governmental organizations
working officially with WHO

**e-mail addresses:**
• for general information on WHO e-mail
**info@who.int**

• for health information, e-mail
**library@who.int**

• for details of publications, e-mail
**publications@who.int**

**Other organizations that fight against
poverty and ill health around the world:**

• Health Unlimited  www.healthunlimited.org

• Health Worldwide www.healthlink.org.uk

• Oxfam            www.oxfam.org.uk

• War on Want      www.gn.apc/waronwant

# Index